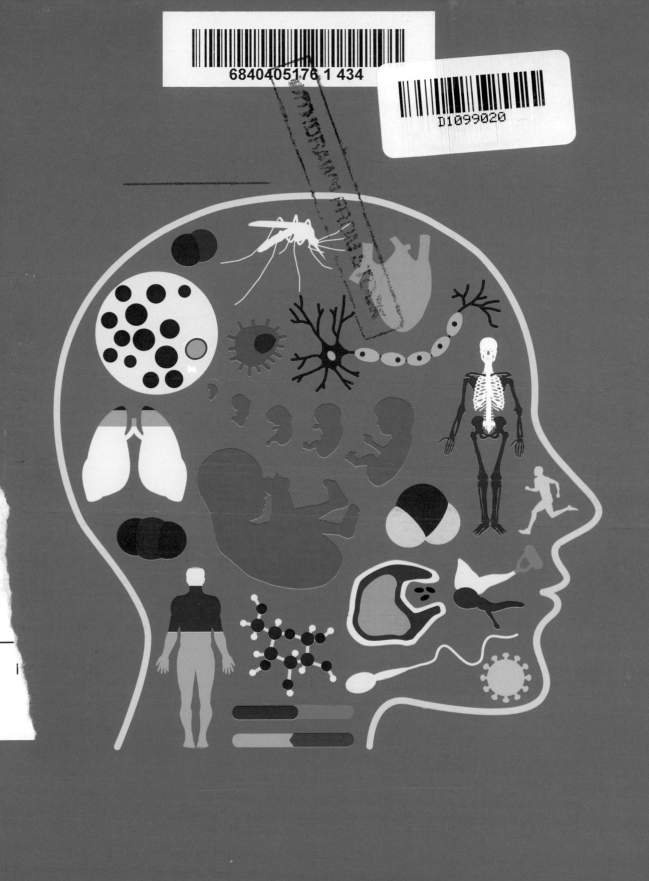

CONTENTS

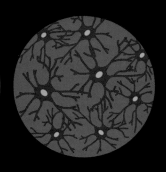
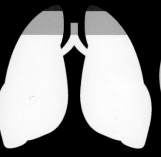

WELCOME TO THE WORLD OF INFOGRAPHICS

Using icons, graphics and pictograms, infographics visualise data and information in a whole new way!

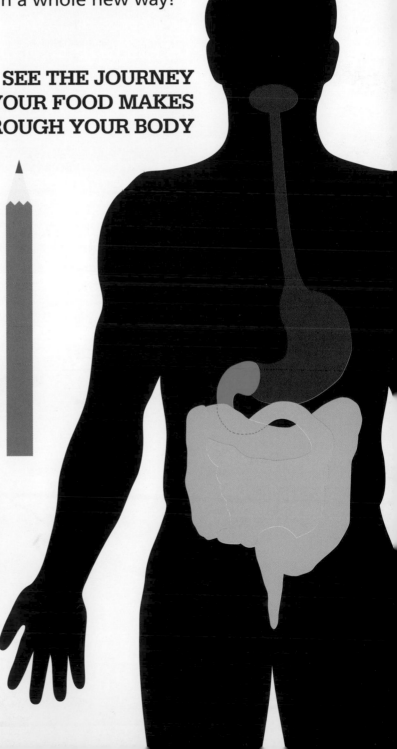

SEE THE JOURNEY YOUR FOOD MAKES THROUGH YOUR BODY

DISCOVER WHAT GOES INTO EVERY DROP OF YOUR BLOOD

SEE HOW MANY PENCILS THE CARBON IN YOUR BODY WOULD FILL

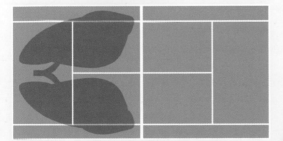

COMPARE YOUR LUNGS' SURFACE AREA TO THAT OF A TENNIS COURT

BUILDING A BODY

The human body is an amazing mixture of tiny structures called cells and a whole host of chemical substances. These cells and substances combine to form a living human being.

CELL SHAPES

Cells are microscopic structures that join together to form larger parts of the human body. Each type of cell is specially shaped to perform a job. Red blood cells are doughnut-shaped so they can carry a lot of oxygen. Sperm cells have long tails so they can swim. Nerve cells are long and thin and have branches to form a network to send messages.

RED BLOOD CELL

SPERM CELL

NERVE CELL

Number of cells in the body

100,000,000,000,000

3,000,000,000 cells die every minute (most of these are replaced).

1.4% NITROGEN

9.5% CARBON

A BODY CONTAINS...

ENOUGH PHOSPHORUS TO MAKE

220

MATCHES

ENOUGH FAT FOR

75

CANDLES

25.5% OXYGEN

ENOUGH CARBON TO FILL # 900 PENCILS

ENOUGH IRON TO MAKE A NAIL THAT'S 7 CM LONG

63% HYDROGEN

HOW THE BODY IS STRUCTURED

Similar types of cell are joined together to form structures called tissues. Different tissues are joined together to create organs and these are linked to create whole body systems.

NERVE CELL

BRAIN

NERVOUS SYSTEM

TINY AMOUNTS OF **CALCIUM, PHOSPHORUS AND POTASSIUM**

NERVE TISSUE

BONE STRUCTURE

The human body keeps its shape thanks to the skeleton, a system of bones that are connected by joints.

SKELETON

The skeleton features a central part called the axial skeleton, made up of the skull, spine and ribs. Off these hang the bones of the limbs, which make up the appendicular skeleton.

A NEWBORN BABY HAS

270

BONES. MANY OF THESE FUSE TOGETHER AND BY ADULTHOOD THERE ARE

206

BONES MAKE UP ABOUT

20%

OF BODY WEIGHT

126 APPENDICULAR BONES

80 AXIAL BONES

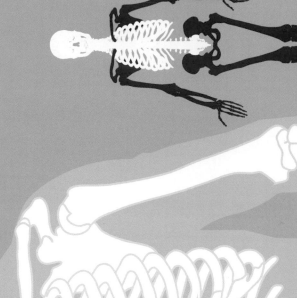

HEALING BONES

Bone tissue has the amazing ability to repair itself when damaged. The process can take as little as a few weeks.

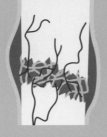

1. Just after the bone breaks, a swelling filled with clotted blood forms around it.

2. Inside the swelling, blood vessels and thin rods of bone start to grow across the break.

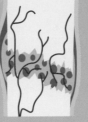

3. More bony tissue grows across the break, forming a hard swollen area called a callus.

4. Bone tissue grows across to heal the break.

FEMUR

FEMUR

ACTUAL SIZE

INCUS

MALLEUS

STAPES

SMALLEST BONES

Found inside the ears, these tiny bones vibrate and carry sounds to the inner ear.

LONGEST BONE

The longest bone in the body is the upper leg bone, or femur. It runs from the hip down to the top of the knee.

50 CM

THERE ARE ABOUT
640
SKELETAL MUSCLES
MAKING UP ABOUT
40%
OF YOUR BODY WEIGHT

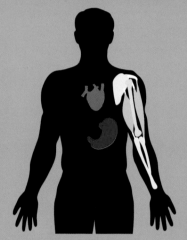

MUSCLES

All the movements that happen in your body, from lifting a leg to raising a smile, are all down to a type of tissue that can contract, called muscle.

MUSCLE TYPES

There are three types of muscle in the body: skeletal, smooth and cardiac. Skeletal muscles move the skeleton, smooth muscles perform a range of tasks, including pushing food through the gut, and the cardiac muscle powers the heart.

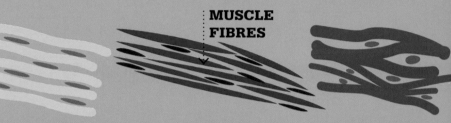

MUSCLE FIBRES

SKELETAL   **SMOOTH**   **CARDIAC**

HOW MUSCLES CONTRACT

Muscles are made up of two types of tiny muscle filament: thick and thin. These tiny muscle filaments slide over each other to make the muscle shorter.

RELAXED MUSCLE

CONTRACTING MUSCLE

FULLY CONTRACTED MUSCLE

THIN FILAMENTS

THICK FILAMENTS

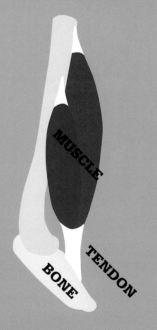

MUSCLE

TENDON

BONE

TENDONS

Skeletal muscles are attached to the bones by thick cords called tendons. The joints themselves are held together by different cords, known as ligaments.

WORKING IN PAIRS

Muscles only exert a force by contracting. This means that they can pull, but cannot push. They need to work in pairs in order to move a body part back and forth. Muscles that work together like this are called antagonistic pairs.

TENDON

BICEPS CONTRACTED

TRICEPS CONTRACTED ·······>

<······ BICEPS RELAXED

TRICEPS RELAXED

TENDON

GLUTEUS MAXIMUS

The name of the largest muscle in the body, found in each buttock.

The **27** bones in your **hand** are controlled by tendons and more than **30** muscles located in the **hand** and **forearm.**

HOW MUCH CAN A MUSCLE MOVE ?

It can be shortened to

85%

CONTRACTED

RELAXED

and stretched to **120%** of its relaxed length.

STRETCHED

ON THE SURFACE

The outside of your body is covered with skin, hair and nails. The skin forms a protective layer, while hair keeps some body parts warm and nails help you to grip objects.

SWEAT GLANDS

Your skin is covered with up to

4 MILLION

sweat glands. The greatest concentrations are found on the palms and the soles where there are up to

350 PER SQ CM.

1 CM
1 CM

SKIN

The largest organ in the human body is the skin. New skin cells form at the bottom of the skin's outer layer. They then move to the surface, die and harden, before flaking off and being replaced.

THERE'S ENOUGH SKIN ON AN ADULT HUMAN TO COVER ABOUT

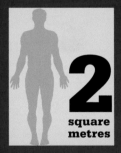

2 square metres

SKIN MAKES UP ABOUT 12% OF YOUR BODY WEIGHT

THAT'S ABOUT

9 KG

IN A 75 KG ADULT

YOU LOSE ABOUT

50,000

flakes of dead skin every minute. That's

18 KG

in a lifetime.

100,000

THE AVERAGE NUMBER OF HAIRS ON THE HUMAN HEAD.

HAIR CAN GROW ABOUT 0.5 MM A DAY. THAT'S **15 MM** IN A MONTH.

15 MM

HAIR

The shape of a person's hair is decided by the shape of the hair's cross-section.

STRAIGHT

WAVY

CURLY

AN ADULT WILL SWEAT ABOUT 0.5 LITRES PER DAY

NAILS

The hard substance that makes up nails is called keratin. It is also found in skin cells and in hair.

CHRISTINE WALTON OF THE USA HAS FINGERNAILS ON BOTH HANDS THAT MEASURE

602 CM

LONG IN TOTAL – THREE TIMES LONGER THAN A VERY TALL PERSON!

BREATHE IN, BREATHE OUT

Oxygen in the air is vital for life. Two sacs, called lungs, inside your chest take oxygen out of the air every time you breathe in.

BREATHING RATES

EXERCISING
80
BREATHS
PER MINUTE

RESTING
15
BREATHS
PER MINUTE

11,000 The number of litres a person will breathe on average each day.

LUNGS HAVE ABOUT 2,400 KM OF AIRWAYS INSIDE THEM. THAT'S THE DISTANCE FROM LONDON TO ATHENS.

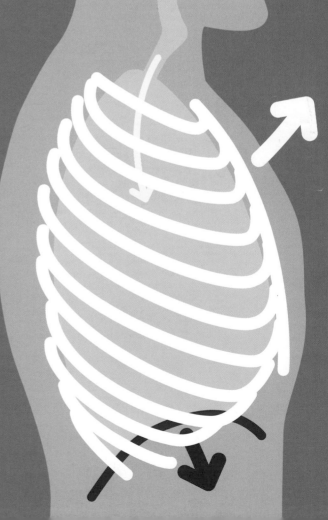

INHALE

The diaphragm contracts and flattens and the muscles between the ribs contract, pulling the ribcage up and out. This draws air into the lungs, through the tubes called airways.

THE SURFACE AREA INSIDE THE LUNGS IS

70 SQUARE METRES

THAT'S THE SAME AS HALF A TENNIS COURT.

THIS LARGE AREA IS CREATED BY UP TO

500,000,000

TINY SAC STRUCTURES, CALLED ALVEOLI

EXHALE

Air flows through the airways until it reaches the alveoli, which are surrounded by tiny blood vessels. The diaphragm and the muscles between the ribs then relax, squeezing air out of the lungs.

ALVEOLI

When air reaches the alveoli, oxygen travels into the blood vessels, while carbon dioxide passes the other way.

WHAT'S IN THE AIR WE BREATHE?

INHALED
79% Nitrogen
20% Oxygen
0.04% CO_2
Tiny amounts of water vapour and various gases

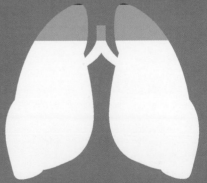

EXHALED
79% Nitrogen
16% Oxygen
4% CO_2, water vapour and other gases

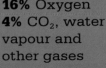

EATING

Running from the mouth to the anus is a long passageway. Its role is to break down the food you eat and take out all the nutrients your body needs to operate, grow and repair itself.

YOUR MOUTH WILL PRODUCE NEARLY

40,000 LITRES

OF SALIVA IN A LIFETIME

THAT'S ABOUT 1–1.5 LITRES EVERY DAY – EQUIVALENT TO SIX GLASSES.

9 METRES

THE LENGTH OF THE ENTIRE DIGESTIVE SYSTEM FROM MOUTH TO ANUS IF STRETCHED OUT STRAIGHT.

FOOD IS CHEWED INSIDE THE MOUTH.

MOUTH

6–10 SECONDS

OESOPHAGUS

1–4 HOURS

THE STOMACH CHURNS AND BREAKS DOWN FOOD TO FORM A MUSH.

STOMACH

LARGE INTESTINE

14 HOURS

2 HOURS

SMALL INTESTINE

4 HOURS

ANUS

YOUR INTESTINES PRODUCE ABOUT 2 LITRES OF GAS EVERY DAY

THE SMALL INTESTINE ABSORBS MOST OF THE NUTRIENTS.

An adult will produce up to

0.25 KG OF POO A DAY.

WHAT'S POO MADE OF?
75% WATER,
25% SOLID MATTER.

Of the solid matter,
30% is dead bacteria,
30% indigestible material (such as cellulose),
10–20% cholesterol and other fats,
10–20% inorganic substances (such as calcium phosphate), and
2–3% proteins.

TEETH
The teeth are covered in a tough substance called enamel, which is the hardest material in the body. Each tooth is shaped to perform a specific job.

MOLAR
GRINDING AND CHEWING

PREMOLAR
GRINDING AND CHEWING

CANINE
PIERCING AND HOLDING

INCISOR
SLICING AND TEARING

PERISTALSIS
Food is pushed through the gut by waves of muscle contractions, called peristalsis.

BLOOD AND THE HEART

THE HEART PUMPS ABOUT 13,640 LITRES OF BLOOD AROUND THE BODY EVERY DAY.

Blood carries oxygen from the lungs and nutrients from the gut to every cell in the body. Here, they are used to produce energy and to repair damaged cells.

HOW MUCH BLOOD?

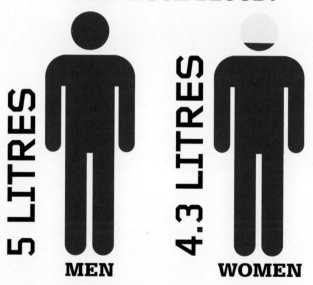

5 LITRES
MEN

4.3 LITRES
WOMEN

YOUR BLOOD CONTAINS UP TO
30,000,000,000
RED BLOOD CELLS

UP TO
2,000,000
ARE MADE EVERY SECOND

WHAT'S IN BLOOD?

Blood is made up of three types of blood cell; red, white and platelets. They all float about in a straw-coloured liquid called plasma.

54.3%
PLASMA

0.7% WHITE CELLS AND PLATELETS

45%
RED BLOOD CELLS

THE HEART

At the heart of the blood system is the heart! This squeezes rhythmically to push blood through the network of tubes, called blood vessels. Each heart beat has four phases.

IN A HEALTHY LIFE, THE HEART WILL BEAT AN AVERAGE 70 BEATS PER MIN – ABOUT 100,000 BEATS PER DAY.

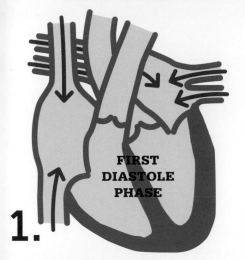

1. FIRST DIASTOLE PHASE

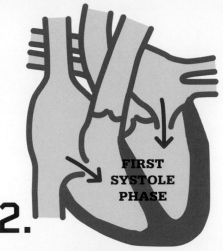

2. FIRST SYSTOLE PHASE

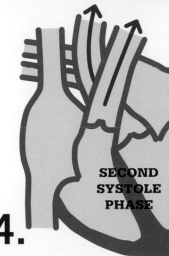

3. SECOND DIASTOLE PHASE

4. SECOND SYSTOLE PHASE

AN ADULT WILL HAVE UP TO **100,000 KM** OF BLOOD VESSELS – ENOUGH TO STRETCH AROUND THE WORLD 2.5 TIMES.

DEFENDING THE BODY

White blood cells help to defend the body from infection and disease. Some of them 'eat up' foreign invaders in a process called phagocytosis.

1. THE CELL SENSES BACTERIA NEARBY AND MOVES TOWARDS THEM

2. THE CELL WRAPS ITS CELL MEMBRANE AROUND THE BACTERIA

3. THE CELL DIGESTS THE BACTERIA

THE SENSES

Sense organs all over your body detect changes in the world around you and send signals to the brain. The organs detect pressure, heat, colours, lights, sounds, tastes and smells.

RANGE OF AUDIBLE SOUND FREQUENCIES IN HERTZ (HZ)

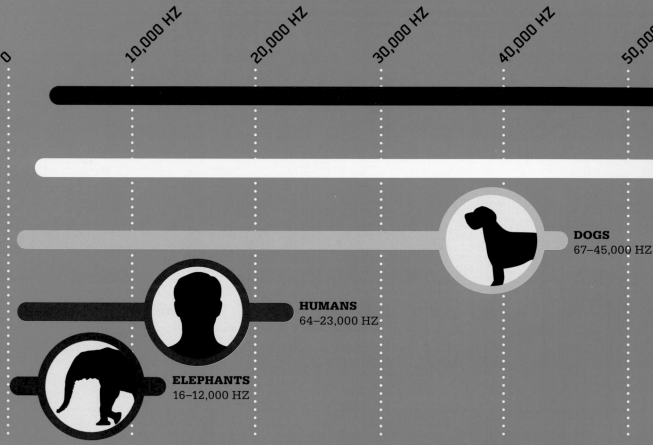

0
10,000 HZ
20,000 HZ
30,000 HZ
40,000 HZ
50,000

DOGS
67–45,000 HZ

HUMANS
64–23,000 HZ

ELEPHANTS
16–12,000 HZ

THE RETINA

The back of the eye is called the retina. It is covered with millions of special cells called rods and cones. Rods detect black and white in low light, while cones can detect all colours in bright light.

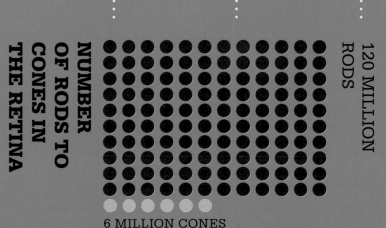

NUMBER OF RODS TO CONES IN THE RETINA

120 MILLION RODS

6 MILLION CONES

18

Your **nose** contains **10–20 million** smell receptor cells and these can detect more than **3,500** different odours.

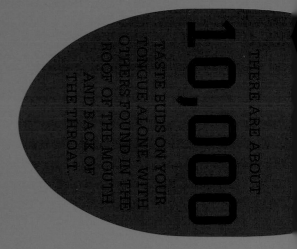

THERE ARE ABOUT **10,000** TASTE BUDS ON YOUR TONGUE ALONE, WITH OTHERS FOUND IN THE ROOF OF THE MOUTH AND BACK OF THE THROAT.

60,000 HZ

70,000 HZ

80,000 HZ

90,000 HZ

100,000 HZ

BATS
2,000–110,000 HZ

MICE
1,000–91,000 HZ

HOW SENSITIVE?

Your skin is packed with touch receptors. These receptors send signals along the nervous system to a part of the brain called the sensory area. Some body parts have more touch receptors than others. This figure shows what you would look like if your body was shaped according to how sensitive each body part was, with the more sensitive parts being the biggest.

YOUR
TONGUE, LIPS AND FINGERS

WOULD BE YOUR BIGGEST PARTS.

WHILE YOUR neck and back WOULD BE VERY SMALL.

19

NERVOUS SYSTEM

Running through your body is a network of nerve fibres. At the centre of this network is the brain, which receives information from your senses and tells the body how to react.

THE BRAIN CONTAINS
1,000,000,000,000
NERVE CELLS

IRONED OUT FLAT, THE OUTER LAYER OF THE BRAIN WOULD COVER
2,090 SQ CM
ABOUT THE AREA OF THREE TENNIS RACKET HEADS

PRIMARY MOTOR AREA
CONTROLS VOLUNTARY MOVEMENTS

ANTERIOR SPEECH AREA
INVOLVED IN PRODUCING SPEECH

SECONDARY MOTOR AREA AND SENSORY AREA
HELPS TO COORDINATE MOVEMENTS

BRAIN GROWTH

INFANT
350 g

1 YEAR
1 KG

PUBERTY
1.3 KG

ADULT
1.5 KG

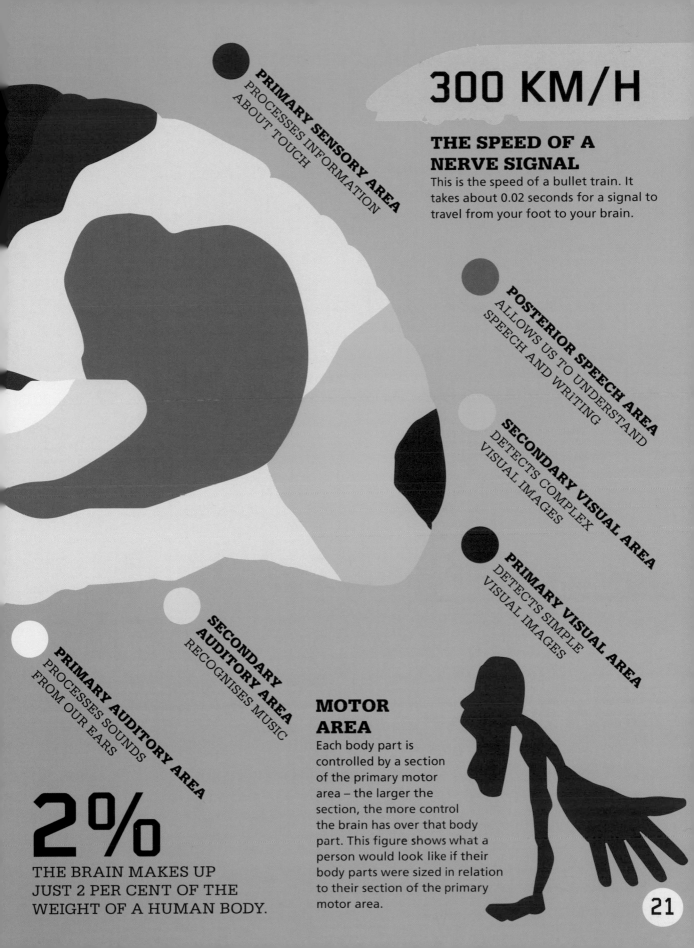

PRIMARY SENSORY AREA
PROCESSES INFORMATION ABOUT TOUCH

300 KM/H

THE SPEED OF A NERVE SIGNAL
This is the speed of a bullet train. It takes about 0.02 seconds for a signal to travel from your foot to your brain.

POSTERIOR SPEECH AREA
ALLOWS US TO UNDERSTAND SPEECH AND WRITING

SECONDARY VISUAL AREA
DETECTS COMPLEX VISUAL IMAGES

PRIMARY VISUAL AREA
DETECTS SIMPLE VISUAL IMAGES

SECONDARY AUDITORY AREA
RECOGNISES MUSIC

PRIMARY AUDITORY AREA
PROCESSES SOUNDS FROM OUR EARS

MOTOR AREA
Each body part is controlled by a section of the primary motor area – the larger the section, the more control the brain has over that body part. This figure shows what a person would look like if their body parts were sized in relation to their section of the primary motor area.

2%
THE BRAIN MAKES UP JUST 2 PER CENT OF THE WEIGHT OF A HUMAN BODY.

21

THE HUMAN HOME

You are not alone! The human body is home to billions of other living organisms, from tiny bacteria to long tapeworms. Some are harmful, but many are essential to your health.

BACTERIA FOUND INSIDE THE GUT OUTNUMBER HUMAN BODY CELLS

HEAD LICE

Head lice are about 3 mm long and feed by biting the scalp and sucking blood through the wound.

 <····· **ACTUAL SIZE**

MALARIA

One of the deadliest diseases, malaria, is caused by Plasmodium parasites in the blood. These parasites are carried by mosquitoes.

10 TO 1

These trillions of bacteria help to break down the chemicals in your food into simpler substances, which you can absorb into your body.

MORE THAN
750,000

PEOPLE DIE FROM MALARIA EVERY YEAR AROUND THE WORLD.

YOUR SKIN IS HOME TO ABOUT **1,000** DIFFERENT SPECIES OF BACTERIA.

600 different species of bacteria live inside a human mouth.

The beef tapeworm can grow up to

12 METRES

long inside the human intestine, the equivalent to the height of seven average-sized adult humans.

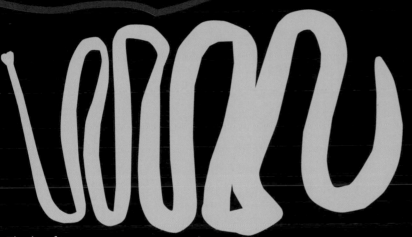

It is thought that there are **500–1,000** different **species** of **bacteria** living in the human **intestine.**

TAPEWORM EGGS HAVE BEEN FOUND IN EGYPTIAN MUMMIES, DATING FROM

2000 BCE

REPRODUCTION

To create a new human being, two tiny cells – a sperm cell from the father and an egg cell (ovum) from the mother – have to meet and fuse together. To do this, the sperm cells need to travel through the uterus and into the correct Fallopian tube.

300,000,000
RELEASED ON AVERAGE AT EJACULATION

NUMBER OF SPERM AT VARIOUS STAGES OF THE JOURNEY TO FERTILIZATION

10,000
ENTER THE UTERUS

3,000 REACH THE TOP OF THE UTERUS

1,500 ENTER THE CORRECT FALLOPIAN TUBE

300 REACH THE OVUM

1 FERTILIZES THE OVUM

RELEASING EGGS

A woman is born with a massive number of egg cells, but only a small proportion of these will develop. Just one is released each month to be fertilised by sperm from a man.

500
START TO DEVELOP AT PUBERTY

1 RELEASED EVERY 28 DAYS

750,000 EGG CELLS PRESENT AT BIRTH

FUSING

Once a sperm reaches the egg cell, it burrows through the egg's outer layers and fuses with the egg.

SPERM

EGG

CELL NUCLEUS

SPERM BURROWS THROUGH OUTER LAYERS

55

The length in micrometres (millionths of a metre) of a human sperm. An egg cell is 120 micrometres across.

GROWING

Soon after fertilisation, the cell starts to divide and form a body. After some time, the cells begin to specialise, creating different body parts, such as fingers and eyes.

35 DAYS

45 DAYS

49 DAYS

56 DAYS

70 DAYS

105 DAYS

GROWING UP

A human will grow until he or she reaches a physical peak, when the body is performing at its best. This is usually at about the age of 25. After that, the body's ability to perform certain tasks starts to decline.

BODY PROPORTION CHANGES

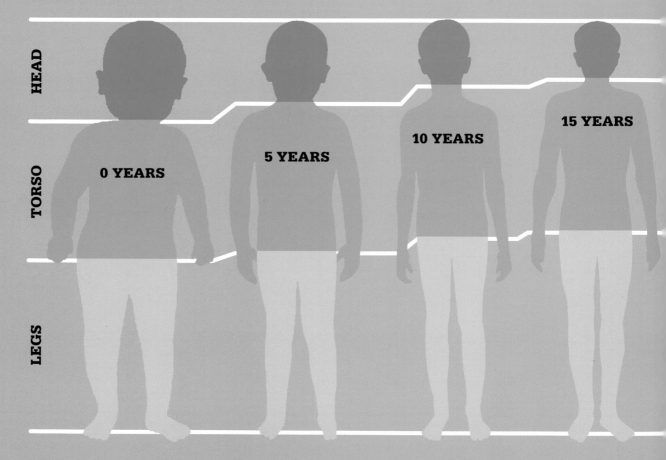

HEAD

TORSO

LEGS

0 YEARS

5 YEARS

10 YEARS

15 YEARS

GROWING BODY

People don't grow at the same rate. There are spurts of growth during puberty. These occur at the ages of about 12 for girls and 14 for boys.

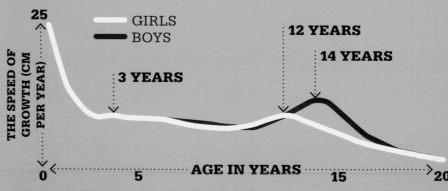

25

THE SPEED OF GROWTH (CM PER YEAR)

GIRLS
BOYS

3 YEARS

12 YEARS

14 YEARS

AGE IN YEARS

0   5   15   20

THE EFFECTS OF AGE...

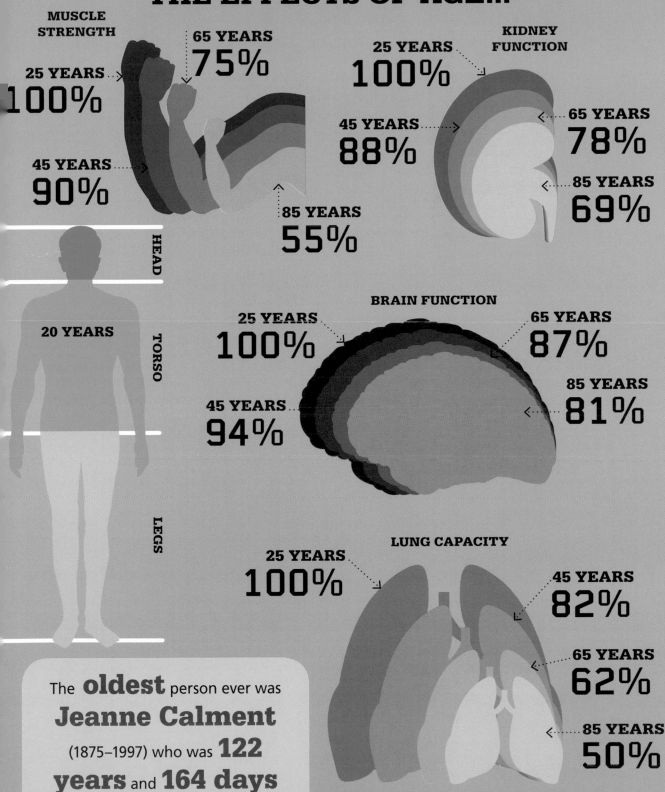

MUSCLE STRENGTH

25 YEARS
100%

65 YEARS
75%

45 YEARS
90%

85 YEARS
55%

KIDNEY FUNCTION

25 YEARS
100%

45 YEARS
88%

65 YEARS
78%

85 YEARS
69%

HEAD

TORSO

LEGS

20 YEARS

BRAIN FUNCTION

25 YEARS
100%

65 YEARS
87%

45 YEARS
94%

85 YEARS
81%

LUNG CAPACITY

25 YEARS
100%

45 YEARS
82%

65 YEARS
62%

85 YEARS
50%

The **oldest** person ever was **Jeanne Calment** (1875–1997) who was **122 years** and **164 days** old when she died.

SPARE PARTS

Body parts wear out or break through injury, disease or old age. Many can be repaired, or, if the damage is serious enough, replaced with natural or artificial parts.

CORNEA
The cornea at the front of the eye can be replaced entirely or in part with a transplant from another person.

COCHLEAR IMPLANT
Also called a bionic ear, this device has microphones to collect sounds and convert them into electrical signals to send to the brain.

LUNGS
A pair of diseased lungs can be replaced with a pair donated by another person.

HEART
A human heart can be transplanted from another person or even from a pig!

PANCREAS
A pancreatic transplant may be carried out on a person suffering from diabetes. It is replaced with a pancreas from a human donor.

KIDNEY
This is the most common form of transplant, where one or both of the kidneys are replaced with kidneys from another person.

LIVER
The liver can be replaced with a whole transplant from a dead person or part of the organ from a living donor.

INTESTINE
Parts of the small or large intestine can be replaced if they have been damaged by disease.

ARTIFICIAL HIP
Metal and ceramic hip pieces replace the worn parts from the leg and hip joint.

PROSTHETIC LIMB

If an arm or leg has to be removed, or amputated, then the whole part can be replaced with a prosthetic limb. Scientists have even developed prosthetic arms and legs that can be controlled by a person's thoughts.

1967

The year of the first heart transplant. It was performed by Christian Barnard at a hospital in Cape Town, South Africa.

2011

The year of the first double leg transplant, performed by a team of surgeons at a hospital in Barcelona, Spain.

BLOOD VESSELS

Blood vessels can be replaced with transplants from another person, or they can be moved and grafted to replace damaged vessels elsewhere in the body.

SKIN

Skin can be taken from one part of the body and grafted to another to cover a serious wound.

TENDONS AND LIGAMENTS

These cord-like structures can be replaced with parts from elsewhere in the body or donations from other people.

BONE MARROW

This is found inside many bones and plays an important role in creating red blood cells. It can be replaced with a donation from another person.

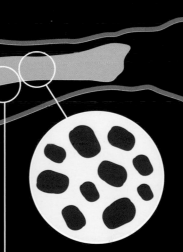

GLOSSARY

amputate
To remove a body part that is diseased or badly damaged.

appendicular skeleton
The part of the skeleton formed by the shoulders, arms, hips and legs.

audible
Something that can be detected by the ear. Different ranges of sound are audible to different animals.

axial skeleton
The central part of the skeleton, formed by the skull, backbone and ribs.

blood vessels
Tubes that carry blood around the body. There are three kinds of blood vessel: arteries, which carry blood from the heart; capillaries, which carry blood from the arteries to individual cells in the body; and veins, which carry blood from the capillaries back to the heart.

cell
The smallest building block of life. All animals and plants are made out of cells. The human body contains about 10 trillion cells.

organ
A group of body tissues that work together to carry out particular jobs in the body. The heart, brain, stomach and skin are all examples of organs in the human body.

contract
To shorten in length. Muscles contract in order to exert a pulling force.

diaphragm
A sheet of muscle that sits across the bottom of the ribs and helps you to breathe.

graft
To move tissue from one part of the body to another. Where a person has badly damaged skin, doctors may graft skin from another part of the body to mend the damaged area.

keratin
A tough substance that is an important part of the skin, nails and hair.

ligaments
Strong, cord-like tissues that connect one bone to another.

muscle filament
Thin strands of muscle tissue that slide over each other when the muscle contracts.

organism
A living thing. An organism may be large, such as a human, or tiny, such as a bacterium.

plasma
A straw-coloured liquid that makes up more than 50 per cent of blood. Red and white blood cells are carried in the plasma.

puberty
A period of body development that starts at around age 12 in girls and 14 in boys. During puberty, the body grows very quickly and changes shape, and the sexual organs develop.

relaxed

A state in which muscles are not exerting a pulling force. Relaxed muscles are longer than muscles that are contracting.

retina

An area at the back of the eye that contains special cells that detect light. The retina sends information to the brain along the optic nerve.

saliva

A watery substance produced inside the mouth. Saliva contains chemicals that start the process of digestion as we chew our food.

phagocytosis

The process by which a cell traps and then destroys bacteria in the body. Some white blood cells kill harmful bacteria by phagocytosis.

species

A group of organisms that are very similar to each other and can reproduce with each other to produce fertile offspring. All living beings belong to one particular species.

system

A group of organs in the body that work together to carry out particular jobs. One organ may work for several different body systems. For instance, the liver works for the digestive system and the circulatory system.

tendons

Strong, cord-like tissues that connect muscles to bones.

tissue

A group of similar cells in the body that does one particular job.

torso

The part of the body to which the limbs and neck are attached. The torso contains most of the body's important organs.

Websites

MORE INFO:
http://www.bbc.co.uk/ science/humanbody/
A guide to the human body from the BBC, containing all kinds of games and tests you can take part in to see how your body works. See how you compare with other people.

kidshealth.org
Answers to all the questions you might have about how your body changes as you grow up.

http://faculty.washington.edu/ chudler/neurok.html
A website packed with fascinating information about the brain for kids and adults.

MORE GRAPHICS:
www.visualinformation.info
A website that contains a whole host of infographic material on subjects as diverse as natural history, science, sport and computer games.

www.coolinfographics.com
A collection of infographics and data visualisations from other online resources, magazines and newspapers

www.dailyinfographic.com
A comprehensive collection of infographics on an enormous range of topics that is updated every single day!

INDEX

ACKNOWLEDGEMENTS

Published in 2013 by Wayland
Copyright © Wayland 2013

Wayland
338 Euston Road
London NW1 3BH

Wayland Australia
Level 17/207 Kent Street
Sydney NSW 2000

All rights reserved.
Senior editor: Julia Adams

Produced by Tall Tree Ltd

Editor: Jon Richards
Designer: Ed Simkins
Consultant: John Clancy

British Library Cataloguing in Publication Data
Richards, Jon, 1970-
   The world in infographics.
   The human body.
   1. Human body--Charts, diagrams, etc.--
   Juvenile literature.
   I. Title II. Human body III. Simkins, Ed.
   612-dc23

ISBN: 9780750278683
Printed in Malaysia

10 9 8 7 6 5 4 3 2 1
Wayland is a division of Hachette
Children's Books, an Hachette UK company.
www.hachette.co.uk

The website addresses (URLs) included in this
book were valid at the time of going to press.
However, because of the nature of the Internet,
it is possible that some addresses may have
changed, or sites may have changed or closed
down, since publication. While the author and
Publisher regret any inconvenience this may
cause the readers, no responsibility for any such
changes can be accepted by either the author
or the Publisher.